COLLECTING THINGS

Kate Needham
Designed by Non Figg

Illustrated by David Eaton • Photographs by Howard Allman
Display ideas: Ray Gibson • Series Editor: Cheryl Evans

Editorial Assistance from Rachael Swann
Additional designs by Lindy Dark

Contents

First published in 1995 by Usborne Publishing Ltd, Usborne House, 83-85 Saffron Hill, London EC1N 8RT, England.
Copyright © 1995 Usborne Publishing Ltd. UE. First published in America in August 1995.
The name Usborne and the device ♥ are Trade marks of Usborne Publishing Ltd. All rights reserved.
No part of this publication may be reproduced, stored in a retrieval system, or transmitted in any form or by any
means, electronic, mechanical, photocopying, recording or otherwise, without the prior permission of the publisher.
Printed in Portugal.

About collecting

You can collect anything you like. Almost everyone has collected something at some point in their lives. Some collections become very valuable, especially as they get older. Some end up in museums. Here are a few things to think about if you start a collection.

What shall I collect?

• Ask people in your family if they have ever collected anything. If they still have the collection perhaps you could start by adding to theirs.

• Choose something that's easy for you to find. It might be shells or pebbles if you live near the sea; stamps or postcards if you have friends who live or travel abroad.

• Collect things that interest you. Find out all you can about them and keep notes.

• You may find that you already have a small collection of things, such as toy cars or china ornaments. You could simply add to this.

Where will I find things?

• Look in junk shops, street markets or charity and second-hand sales for older items.

• Try swapping or trading spare items with friends.

• Join a club to find out more about your hobby and meet people to trade with.

• Look in specialist magazines for advertisements of clubs and news about swap meets.

• Tell other people what you have decided to collect. Collections grow more quickly with lots of people looking for things instead of just one.

Storage and display

You will find lots of ideas for displaying the things you collect in this book. It is fun to show them off but here are a few things to remember if you want to keep a collection in good condition:

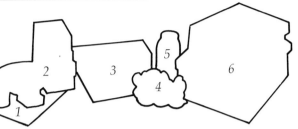

• Avoid handling things too much - it makes them dirty. Use tweezers or hold them by the edges.
• Things displayed in sunlight tend to fade. Display them away from the window, or keep them in a box.
• Scrap books or files with individual plastic folders prevent paper collections from getting ripped, creased or scratched.

You could collect different boxes and trays to keep things in. Paint and label them to use for display. See the photograph below, and the key to it on the right, for ideas.

1. Files are useful for paper collections which need to be kept flat.
2. Use various small boxes for different-sized parts of your collection.
3. Chocolate boxes have ready-made compartments that are ideal for sorting small collections in.
4. You can spray egg cartons gold or silver. Line them with bright tissue paper and display fragile items inside.
5. With glass jars you can see what's inside.
6. Shoe boxes are a useful size and they stack up easily. Add a label to the front, saying what's inside.

Stamps

Lots of people collect stamps. It's cheap and easy to start and you could build up a valuable collection. This hobby is called philately.

Where to get stamps

Start by collecting all the stamps that come on your letters. Ask friends, relations or anyone you know abroad to keep stamps for you too.

You can buy cheap packs of stamps from a stationery or stamp shop. Keep the ones you want and swap the others with a friend.

Post offices regularly bring out special editions of stamps. Find out what they are and buy the ones you like.

The country collections above are from Tanzania, India, Australia and Switzerland.

These thematic collections show industry, animals, transportation and flowers.

Getting stamps off an envelope

If you want your stamps to be valuable, it is important not to damage them when you take them off the envelope. Here is the best way to do this.

1. Cut around the stamp. Take care not to cut the perforations - the jagged parts at the edge of the stamp.

2. Float it face down in a bowl of warm water for about 20 minutes. This helps to loosen the glue.

3. Peel the stamp from the paper. If it doesn't come off easily, leave it to soak and try again later.

4. Put the stamps on kitchen paper to dry. Leave plenty of space between them or they will stick together.

Organizing your collection

Once you've collected quite a few stamps, it's a good idea to divide them up into countries or themes. You may decide to collect stamps from just one country or of just one theme, such as animals and flowers.

Most stamps have the country they come from written on them. British stamps, however, do not because they were the first ones. They have the Queen's head instead.

Stamp errors

Look for stamps with printing mistakes. They can be quite valuable. Here are some mistakes you could look for:

- upside down writing or picture
- writing or picture is left off
- the wrong ink is used
- spelling mistakes

Spare stamps

You may soon find that you have several of the same stamps. Keep the best one and try to swap the others. Spare ones with no value, can be used to decorate album covers, or containers for storing equipment, like this:-

For a pen holder, use a round cardboard container. Paint it inside and out.

Glue stamps on in a random pattern, using a glue stick. Varnish if you like - see page 15.

Albums and useful equipment

The first thing you need for a stamp collection is an album to keep it in. To place stamps in it, you will need hinges or mounts. You can buy these, and the other useful things in the picture, from stationery or stamp shops. Write a heading for each part of your collection. You can find out how to letter headings on the next page.

Stamp hinges are for putting stamps in an album. Find out how to use them over the page.

With loose-leaf albums you can add pages as your collection grows.

Mounting strips can be added to a page or cut up to use for individual stamps.

A magnifiying glass is useful to study detail.

Use tweezers to keep stamps clean.

Some albums come with headings and pictures.

Lettering headings

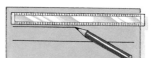

1. Using a ruler, draw a line on the page, where you want your heading to be. Then draw another one ½cm (¼in) above it.

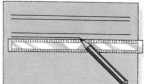

2. Draw two more lines, one 3mm (⅛in) below the first, the other 3mm (⅛in) above the second. This makes a grid to write in.

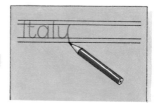

3. Write your heading in pencil. Make tall letters, like "l" or "t", and capitals, reach the top line. Make letters with tails, like "y", reach the bottom line.

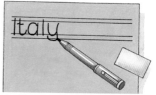

4. Go over the writing with a felt-tip pen. Let it dry, then remove the pencil lines with an eraser.

"Commemoratives" are issued on special occasions, such as the Channel Tunnel opening.

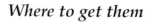

Telephone cards

People have been collecting stamps for more than 150 years but telephone cards are quite new. The first ones appeared in Italy in 1975. People started collecting them immediately. The hobby is sometimes called fusilately. Like stamps, cards have all kinds of pictures and come from lots of different countries.

Some cards advertise a product. Others are made for a special event.

Where to get them

All kinds of places sell telephone cards. Look for a sign in the window.

The best way to get hold of used ones is to ask friends and relatives to keep them for you. If you know someone who is going abroad, ask them to bring back a foreign one.

Look in a telephone card magazine for addresses of fairs and clubs where you can trade your cards with other collectors. You can also find out from these magazines when special series of cards are being issued.

Storing cards

It is important to store your cards carefully so that they don't get dirty or scratched. You can buy special albums with transparent pockets, or you could make a filing box, see opposite.

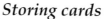

Placing stamps in an album

1. Fold over the top of a stamp hinge. Lick the folded part with your tongue.

2. Press the folded part onto the back of the stamp, in the middle, near the top.

3. Lick the back of the hinge, and position the stamp on your album page.

4. Use a clean sheet of paper to press against it so that the hinge sticks firmly.

"Definitives" are everyday stamps. Their shade and size varies according to the value.

Lots of countries issue special stamps for Christmas.

Filing box

This box will be just the right size for your telephone cards.
You need: a 20 x 30cm (8 x 12in) piece of thin cardboard; scissors; glue stick; a ruler; a hard pencil.

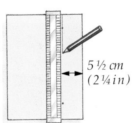

5 ½ cm (2¼ in)

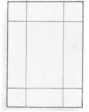

1. Draw a line 5½cm (2¼in) in from one side. Mark two dots first to help you make a straight line.

2. Do the same on the three other sides, so that your card looks like the picture above.

3. Score along all the lines. To do this, place a ruler along the line and go over it again, pressing very firmly.

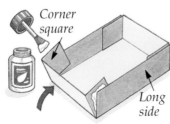

Corner square

Long side

Tab

Decorate with bright paper or felt-tip pens.

4. Cut along the lines marked red in the picture. Then fold up all the sides along the lines you scored.

5. Put glue on each corner square. Then glue each corner square inside the long sides.

6. For a divider, draw around a telephone card. Add a 4 x 1cm (1½ x ½in) tab for the label and cut out.

Postcards

Postcards are easy to collect because there are so many of them. The first thing is to decide what type of card you want to collect.

Topographic cards

Cards with views of places are called topographic cards. Ask friends and relatives to send them to you when they go away.

You could send postcards to yourself when you go away. Choose unusual views, as they may be more valuable in years to come. If you like, keep a map and mark on it where all your cards come from.

Thematic cards

You might prefer to collect by theme, such as cards with cats or planes.

If you like art, you could collect cards of famous paintings. Art galleries always have a good selection.

Old cards

The first picture postcards appeared at the turn of this century when few people had telephones. They sent cards with messages instead. The message was often written on the picture.

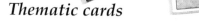

Lots of people collected cards in those days, which means you can still find plenty of old ones. You can buy them at postcard fairs or in some flea markets. Some are quite expensive.

If you find an old card, compare it with a modern one of the same place and see how things have changed.

Trafalgar Square, London, 1990s.

Trafalgar Square, London, 1900s.

Concertina display

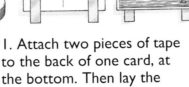

You can join postcards together with masking tape. This peels off easily without damaging the cards.

1. Attach two pieces of tape to the back of one card, at the bottom. Then lay the card flat, picture side up.

2. Place the top edge of another card exactly along the bottom edge of the first. Press down firmly so it sticks to the tape.

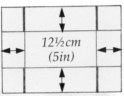

3. Add as many cards as you want. Tape some ribbon to the top and hang on the wall.

When you want to change your display, fold it up and store it in a box (see below).

Tape a label to the top card. When you file it away, this will act as a divider.

Storing cards

Store cards in a filing box like the one on page 7. Change the size as follows:

Use a 50 x 42½cm (20 x 17in) rectangle of thin cardboard. Draw lines at 12½cm (5in).

For the divider, draw around a postcard. Add space for a label, then cut out.

12½cm (5in)

Tower display

1. Attach tape to the sides of a card. Join four or more together in a circle.

2. Stack the circles on top of each other. See how high a tower you can make.

9

Marbles

The game of marbles has been around since Roman and Greek times. The earliest marbles were made of stone, marble or clay. Later some were made from precious stones. Nowadays marbles are made of glass with all kinds of patterns. Many of them have special names. You can see some of the popular ones on this page.

Cat's eyes

Turtles

Chinas

Lustered chinas

Clays

Superstars

To start a collection, buy a few marbles from a toy shop. Add to it by learning to play and winning marbles from friends. There are three types of game, one of each is shown below, but first you need to learn how to shoot.

How to shoot

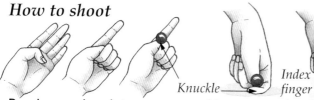

Knuckle *Index finger*

Bend your thumb into your hand. Wrap three fingers around it. Place a marble onto your thumb knuckle.

Use your index finger to hold it there. Place the knuckle of your index finger on the ground and flick out your thumb.

What's a "tolley"

A "tolley" is the marble you shoot with. It is usually bigger than the others. Try several marbles until you find one the right size.

The tolley used in the games below looks like this.

Ringer:- knock marbles out of a ring.

Start by drawing a circle on the ground. Place 13 marbles inside it, in the shape of a cross.

Shoot from the edge of the ring. Score one point for every marble you knock out.

If you knock a marble out of the circle, take an extra turn from where your tolley stops.

Potsies:- shoot your marble into a hole.

Choose a hole to aim for.

Grooves

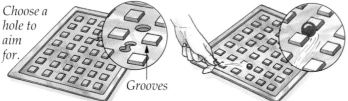

Other player's tolley

First find a hole to shoot into. A manhole cover in the playground is good. You have to aim between the grooves.

Take turns to shoot. Start from the edge of the cover, then play each shot from where your tolley stops.

Once you reach the hole, use your turn to shoot at the other tolleys. Each time you hit one, you win a marble.

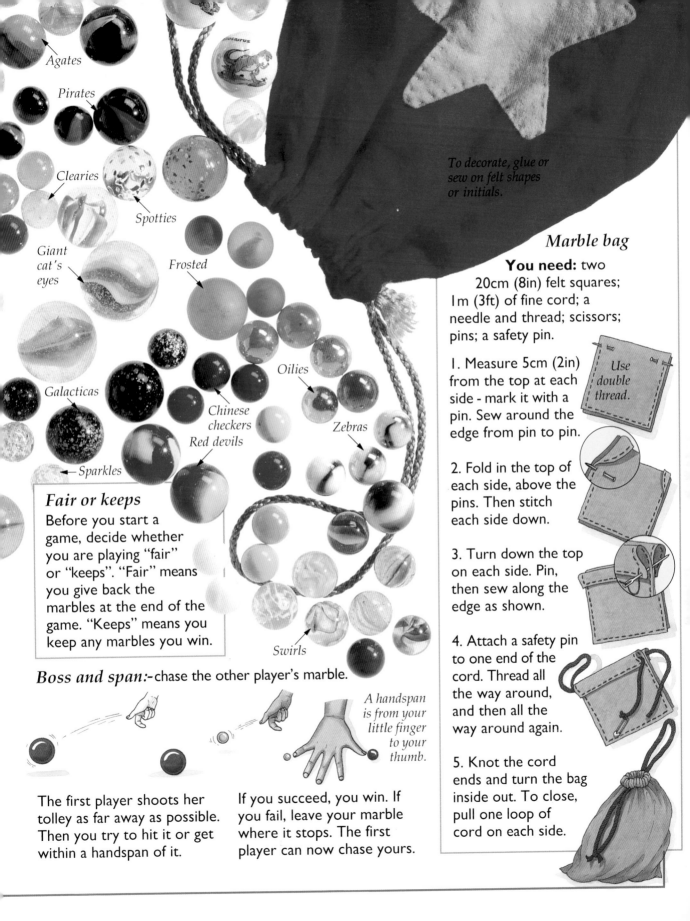

Agates

Pirates

Clearies

Spotties

Giant cat's eyes

Frosted

Galacticas

Chinese checkers

Red devils

Oilies

Zebras

Sparkles

Swirls

To decorate, glue or sew on felt shapes or initials.

Marble bag

You need: two 20cm (8in) felt squares; 1m (3ft) of fine cord; a needle and thread; scissors; pins; a safety pin.

Use double thread.

1. Measure 5cm (2in) from the top at each side - mark it with a pin. Sew around the edge from pin to pin.

2. Fold in the top of each side, above the pins. Then stitch each side down.

3. Turn down the top on each side. Pin, then sew along the edge as shown.

4. Attach a safety pin to one end of the cord. Thread all the way around, and then all the way around again.

5. Knot the cord ends and turn the bag inside out. To close, pull one loop of cord on each side.

Fair or keeps

Before you start a game, decide whether you are playing "fair" or "keeps". "Fair" means you give back the marbles at the end of the game. "Keeps" means you keep any marbles you win.

Boss and span:- chase the other player's marble.

A handspan is from your little finger to your thumb.

The first player shoots her tolley as far away as possible. Then you try to hit it or get within a handspan of it.

If you succeed, you win. If you fail, leave your marble where it stops. The first player can now chase yours.

Badges

Some badges advertise a product.

Some badges advertise a product.

The cheapest badges to collect are tin badges. These were invented at the turn of the century and were first produced by button manufacturers which is why they are sometimes called "pin back buttons" or "button badges".

Enamel badges have been around much longer. They are more valuable and are made in all kinds of shapes.

Small enamel badges with a spike on the back are sometimes called pin badges. Many people collect just these.

Others have a serious message, or a silly one.

Some say how old you are.

Make your own badge

You need: white paper; thin cardboard; pens; glue stick; scissors; self-adhesive plastic; strong tape; a safety pin.

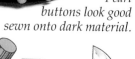

Pin badges or sew buttons onto clothes.

Pearl buttons look good sewn onto dark material.

Simple shapes are easier to cut out.

HELLO

HELLO

1. Draw a badge design on white paper and decorate it.

2. Add a message. Then glue the design onto thin cardboard.

3. Cover with self-adhesive plastic and then cut it out.

You could use a magazine picture of a popstar or sports player.

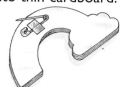

HELLO

4. Glue the badge onto more thin cardboard and cut it out again.

5. Do this several times to make a nice strong badge. Tape on a small safety pin.

Try a picture of a pet.

Club badge

If you like, you could set up your own collectors club with friends. Give it a name and make a special badge for each of the members.

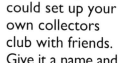

Buttons

Buttons have been used for thousands of years. The Ancient Greeks used them to fasten their tunics at the shoulder.

In Europe they were first used just for decoration. When buttonholes were invented, in the 13th century, they became so popular that laws were passed to limit their use.

For old buttons, look in flea markets and rummage sales. Ask your grandparents if they have kept a button box. Check out second-hand clothes shops to see if any garments are worth buying just for the buttons.

Buttons can be made of all kinds of things, such as wood, brass, horn, bone, leather, mother of pearl or plastic.

Elaborate, 17th century clothes had hundreds of buttons.

Sew buttons into a pattern.

Remember to remove badges before you wash the clothes, or they may rust.

Small buttons are often sold on cards.

Make your own buttons

You need: thin cardboard; scissors; oven-hardening clay (e.g. Fimo®); rolling pin; foil; baking tray; craft knife; cocktail stick.

Add stripes or spots of another shade.

Or mix clays for a marble effect.

1. Draw and cut out a cardboard pattern for the button.

2. Check that it fits through the buttonhole.

Push in from each side and twist around.

3. Roll out some clay in a flat piece, about 4mm (¼in) thick.

4. Press the pattern onto the clay. Cut around it. Repeat for each button.

5. Use a cocktail stick to make two holes in the middle of each button.

Varnish when cool.

6. Lay the buttons on a foil-covered tray and bake according to the instructions.

Secret buttons

In 1545, the king of France sent two secret letters to captains in England. They were sewn inside two special buttons made of silk thread.

Shells

You can find shells on almost every seashore. They are made by small creatures which live in them. When these creatures die, their shells are washed up on the shore.

Only collect empty shells. The creatures that live in them will die if you take them away from the sea.

When to look

The best time to hunt for shells is at low tide. This is when the sea is farthest out. Be careful of the tide. It can come in very fast and cut off your route home.

A line of seaweed at the top of the beach shows where the last tide came to. It is a good place for shells.

Try looking for shells after a storm. Large waves bring bigger shells onto the beach.

Sorting your collection

Scientists divide shells into classes and families. The two most common classes are "gastropods", which are single shells and are often coiled, and "bivalves", which come in pairs with a little hinge. Look for ones that are still attached.

Families are groups of shells with similar features. On the left are lots of different shells from all over the world. Try to identify your shells from these. Use a book from the library if you can't find your shell here.

Find out how to make these plaques over the page.

Scallop shells make nice bowls to keep things in. Ask your fishmonger if he has any.

Spider conch

Cat's paw scallop

Prickly cockle

Wentletraps

Cone shells

Oysters

Top shells

Violet sea snails

Tiger cowrie

Serpent's head cowries

Moon shells

Jingle shells

Calico clam

Venus clams

Coquina clams

Beautiful tellin

Limpets

Razor shells

Watermelon tellins

Queen scallops

Mussels

Common whelks

Abalones

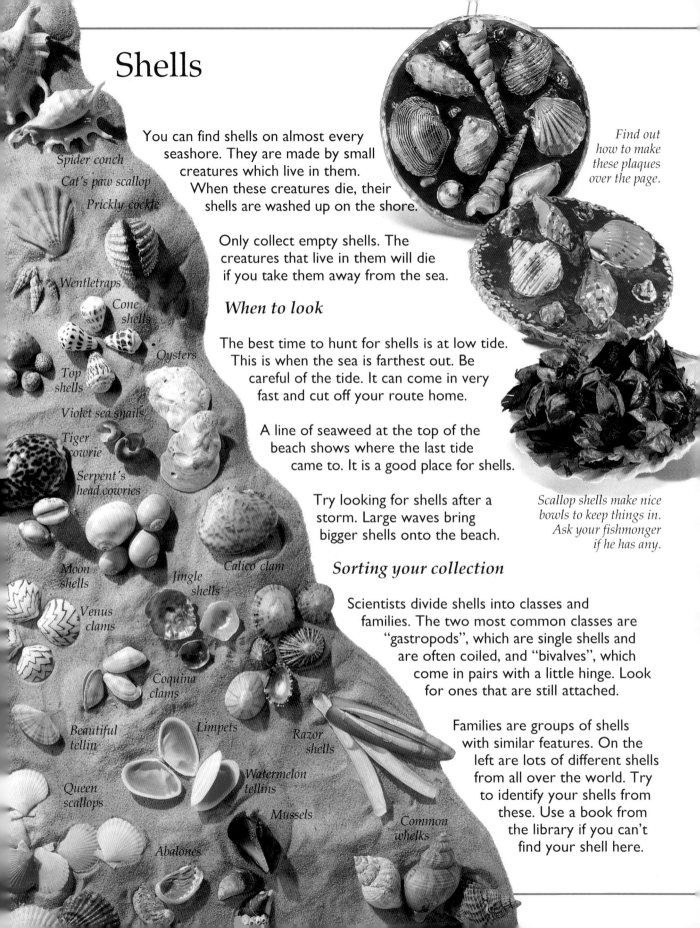

How to collect

Take a bucket, plastic bags, pen and paper. Put each unusual shell in a separate bag with a label saying where you found it.

When you get home, soak your shells in warm, soapy water. Use a toothbrush to scrub them clean very gently.

Store delicate shells in a box lined with tissue or soft material. You could display larger ones on a tray like the one on page 19.

Tip

To keep bivalves in pairs, wrap some thread around them while they dry.

Decorating with shells

You can use shells to decorate all sorts of things, such as boxes, jars and mirror or picture frames.

You need: shells; something to decorate; PVA (household) glue, which dries clear.

1. Before you start, make sure that the surface you want to decorate is clean and dry. Then arrange the shells on it.

2. Pick up one shell at a time. Add glue and press it back into place. When all the shells are glued on, varnish as explained below.

Decorate the lid of a jar and fill it with bath pearls for a present.

Varnishing

Add shells to an old picture frame.

Use small shells to decorate a plain hair clip.

You can make your own varnish by mixing PVA glue with water. Use two measures of glue and one of water. Mix them together thoroughly.

Make sure the shells are dry. Brush varnish all over them. Leave to dry and then repeat. When you have finished, wash your brushes in cold water.

Make a shell plaque

This is a good decoration to make without using up your best shells. You can use one shell to make all the prints, or several different ones.

You need: a cake tin or plastic box; plastic food wrap; plaster of Paris; petroleum jelly; modelling clay or playdough; medium or small shells; a paper clip.

Pebbles

Other things to collect from the seashore are pebbles. Pebbles are pieces of rock that have broken off and been worn smooth by water. They vary in shape and size, according to the rock they come from. You can see a few types here. A geologist at your local museum can help you find out more about your pebbles.

Above: brick

Below: fossils in limestone

Above: glass

Below: calcite vein

1. Line the tin with food wrap. Press clay all over the base. Make sure the clay is deeper than the shells you plan to use.

2. Wipe the shells with jelly. Press them upside down into the clay. Take them out carefully, to leave a clear impression.

It should be like thick yogurt.

Stir thoroughly until it is creamy.

It takes about 30 minutes to dry completely.

3. Ask an adult to help mix the plaster. For a cake tin use about ½ kilo (¾lb) of plaster and ¼ litre (½ pint) of cold water.

4. Pour the plaster all over the clay. Then tap the edges of the tin to get rid of any air bubbles that may have formed.

5. Push one end of the paper clip into the plaster. Hold until it starts to set. This will make a hook to hang the plaque with.

6. When dry, turn it out of the tin. Pull off the food wrap and the clay. Scrub clean under cold water. Paint and varnish it to finish.

Faces in a jar

Pebbles are fun to paint. Ones with hollows or bumps can easily be turned into faces. Paint lots and arrange them so that they look out of a jar.

Use larger pebbles as paperweights, or you could collect pebbles with holes in them. Display them on a string.

For tips on painting pebbles follow the instructions for the cat paperweight below.

Use hollows for eyes or a mouth. Lumps can be noses or chins.

Keep natural pebbles in water to make them look bright.

Cat paperweight

You need: a large pebble; acrylic or poster paints; a fine paint brush; varnish - see page 15.

1. Paint the pebble with a base coat of white paint. Leave to dry. Then paint it with yellow paint and leave to dry again.

2. Paint an outline for the head and tail with a fine brush. Paint on eyes, nose and a mouth. Add orange and white markings.

3. Paint on several orange stripes for the body. Leave to dry and then varnish.

Below: flints

Right: pebble made of marble fragments

Below: quartz veins

Tip

Only handle when cool.

To make paint dry faster, place the stone on foil in a low oven for a few minutes.

17

Fossils

Fossils are some of the oldest things you can collect. They are the shapes of living things left in the rock millions of years ago.

How a fossil is made

A fossil begins to be made when a dead animal or plant gets covered with sand or mud.

Gradually, over thousands of years, the mud turns to rock and the shape of the animal or plant is preserved.

When the rock gets worn away by the sea and weather, the fossil shows on the surface. This is why cliffs near the sea are a good place to find them.

Some rocks are full of fossils, while others have none. To discover the best places to find fossils near you, ask in your local library or museum. You can also buy fossils at seaside places and in museums.

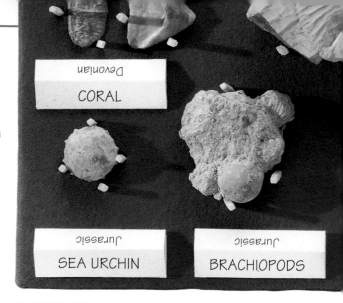

Devonian
CORAL

Jurassic
SEA URCHIN

Jurassic
BRACHIOPODS

What fossils tell us

People who study fossils are called paleontologists. By studying fossils and the rocks they are found in, they can discover many things about life on Earth before people existed. Everything we know about dinosaurs is from studying fossils.

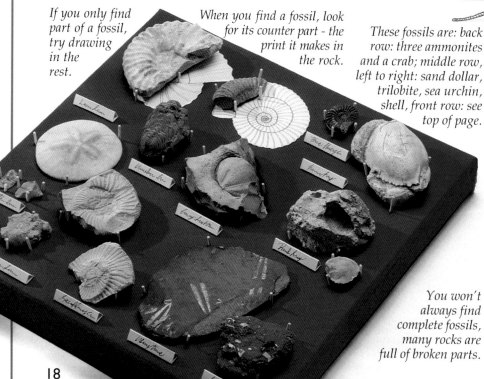

If you only find part of a fossil, try drawing in the rest.

When you find a fossil, look for its counter part - the print it makes in the rock.

These fossils are: back row: three ammonites and a crab; middle row, left to right: sand dollar, trilobite, sea urchin, shell, front row: see top of page.

You won't always find complete fossils, many rocks are full of broken parts.

Collecting tips

• As a beginner, only collect fossils that are loose on the ground.
• Take newspaper to wrap each fossil in, pencil and paper to write down where and when you found it, and a plastic bag.
• When you get home, look up your find in a book. What kind of animal or plant was it? How old is it?
• Pack your fossils carefully in a box or drawer, or display them as shown here.

AMMONITE — Jurassic

GRAPTOLITES — Paleozoic

BIVALVE SHELLS — Pleistocene

Pizza box display tray

You need: a large pizza box; newspaper; a craft knife; used matchsticks; felt; a pen; tape.

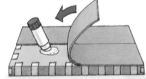

1. Fill the box with crumpled paper. Then tape it closed. Tape over the corners too.

2. Glue felt to the top and sides of the box. Cut several pieces and join them neatly.

3. Arrange the fossils on top. Mark several dots around each one, close to its base.

4. Remove the fossils. With the craft knife, make a tiny cross cut on each dot.

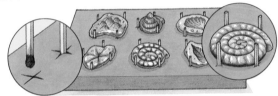

5. Push a matchstick, used end down, into each hole. Leave 1cm (½in) showing.

6. Put the fossils back. The matchsticks will hold them in place when the tray moves.

For the labels

For each label you need a piece of stiff white paper, 6 x 10cm (2½ x 4in).

1. Fold the paper carefully in half, short edges together. Open back out.

2. Fold each short edge into the middle. Open back out and turn the paper over.

3. Print the name of your fossil very neatly in section three. See page 6 for tips on lettering.

4. Turn the paper upside down. Add any other information, such as where and when you found it, or how old it is, in section two.

5. Add glue to section one. Fold the label into a triangle shape, as shown, and glue section four to section one.

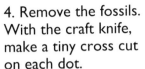

Make a leaf fossil

Follow the instructions for the shell plaque on page 16 but instead of pushing a shell into the playdough, use a leaf and leave it there. Remove it at the end with the playdough.

Miniatures

A miniature can be anything that is small. Small things are good to collect because they don't take up too much room. This means you can easily display them on a window sill, or store them away in a box.

The step-by-step instructions opposite show you how to make some small display shelves for miniatures but first you must choose what to collect. You will find lots of ideas on this page.

On the display shelves are clockwork toys and cars.

On the mirrors below are dinosaurs, Christmas decorations and erasers.

These key rings are all shoes but you can find all kinds of themes to collect. Use pins to display them on a board.

Pencil ends are small and cheap. Display them on pencils in a mug or jar.

Miniature shelves

You need: three (or more) long boxes - the type that plastic food wrap or kitchen foil come in are ideal; tape; scissors; a felt-tip pen; glue stick and felt (or you could buy self-adhesive felt).

1. Tape over any sharp, serrated edges on the boxes. Then tape two of the boxes together.

2. Tape the third box on top of one of the others, so that it makes a step, as shown.

3. Stand the boxes on the felt, as shown. Draw around the end carefully with the felt-tip pen.

4. Cut out the shape you just drew and glue it onto one end. Do the same for the other end.

5. Cut pieces of felt to cover the top and side of each shelf and for the back. Then glue them on.

6. Cut a piece of cardboard to fit the back. Tape and glue it on firmly, then cover it in felt.

7. For taller display shelves, glue three more boxes together. Then add them to the back.

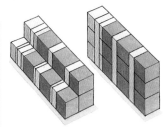

8. For wider display shelves, make two sets. Glue them together firmly at the sides.

Mirror display

Mirrors are a great way to show off different objects because they reflect all sides of them.

These mirrors show a collection of various china ornaments. You could collect just one type.

You need: mirror tiles, which you can buy in hardware stores; jar lids; bright tape.

Tape around the edges of the tiles. Then place the tiles on the jar lids and arrange your collection on them.

Other popular miniatures to collect are cartoon characters from an animated film.

Souvenirs

If you go away on a long trip or even just for the day, it can be fun to collect souvenirs. These are things that remind you of the place you went to.

You could also collect souvenirs about a hobby, team or band that you particularly like.

A souvenir can be absolutely anything - a ticket, a postcard, a baseball cap or a leaf from a tree. On the right are some ideas for the things you could collect.

Football club

Collect: headlines and pictures from newspapers and magazines; tickets; badges; autographs of the players; team scarf.

Pop band

Collect: pictures of the players; CD covers; fan club letters; concert tickets; autographs; titles of the best songs.

Party

Collect: invitation; cards; food wrappers; photographs; paper napkin; balloons; cake decorations; gift tags; bows from presents.

Wedding

Collect: photographs; cake decorations; confetti; pressed flower from bouquet; name card; invitation.

For a trip away, collect tickets; postcards; photographs; shells; badges; coins.

Souvenir board

You could keep your souvenirs in a scrap book, but if you want to show them off, try making this board for the wall.

You need: souvenirs; a large piece of strong cardboard; bright paper; sharp scissors; thin cardboard; small cans and boxes; ruler; glue stick; PVA (household) glue.

1. Cut the paper to the same size as the strong cardboard. Arrange the pictures and anything else you want to frame, on it. Leave space for a title at the top.

2. For each thing you want to frame, choose a box or tin that is slightly smaller. Place it on the paper where you want the picture to go, and draw around it carefully.

3. For star or heart shapes, use some thin cardboard folded in half. Draw half the shape against the fold, then cut it out.

4. Unfold the cardboard and draw around it. When you have drawn a shape for each picture, you can cut them out. Do it carefully, like this:

First push the point of the scissors into the middle of the shape. Then cut to the line you drew. Snip around it, a little piece at a time.

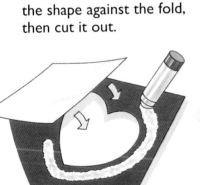

5. Glue the pictures behind the frames with glue stick. When they are dry, turn the paper over and glue it firmly onto the piece of strong cardboard.

6. To finish, decorate the edges of each frame with any remaining souvenirs, such as shells or coins. Then give your collection a title and add the date of the trip or event.

If you like, add a sand or glitter pattern. Paint on the pattern with glue stick first, then sprinkle on the sand or glitter. Shake off any excess onto newspaper.

Autographs

An autograph is someone's signature. You can collect autographs from friends or from famous people.

Some people keep an autograph book. You can buy these at stationers', or use a small pad with plain paper and decorate the cover. Tie a pen to it with thread or fine ribbon, so that there will always be something to sign with.

You might not always have your autograph book with you, particularly if you just happen to spot a famous person. Use any piece of paper and add it to your book later. You could add a photograph of the person next to it.

Baseball bat and ball with players' autographs

At concerts or plays, you might get the chance to go back stage. Take your ticket, album cover or a poster with you and ask to have it signed.

If you want a special autograph you could write and ask for it. Pop groups and football clubs usually have fan clubs you can write to.

Elaborate autographs

Some people have very elaborate autographs.

This is how Queen Elizabeth I signed herself.

Try some ideas for your own original autograph. Find one you like then perfect it.

Autograph T-shirt

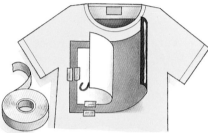

Why not collect the autographs of a band or football team and copy them onto a T-shirt, or ask players to sign an object directly.

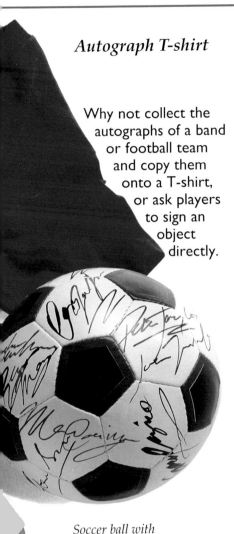

Soccer ball with autographs of a local team

You need: a clean, ironed T-shirt; fabric pens or paint; cardboard; carbon paper; tape; a ballpoint pen; a clear copy of the autograph.

1. Lay the shirt flat and put a piece of cardboard inside it, where you want the autograph to go.

3. Go over the letters of the autograph with a ballpoint pen. Press down hard. Then remove the carbon paper.

You may want to enlarge an autograph first. You can do this quite easily and cheaply on a photocopier. Ask someone to show you how.

2. Tape the carbon paper, ink side down, onto the shirt. Tape the copy of the autograph onto the carbon paper.

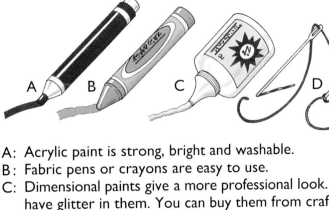

4. The autograph should have transferred to the shirt. Go over it with fabric pens or paint. See below for ideas.

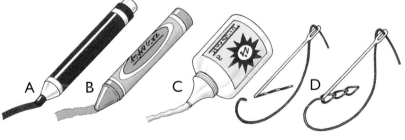

A: Acrylic paint is strong, bright and washable.
B: Fabric pens or crayons are easy to use.
C: Dimensional paints give a more professional look. Some have glitter in them. You can buy them from craft shops.
D: You could embroider over the signature.

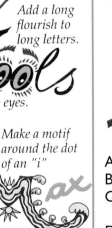

Add a long flourish to long letters.

Turn "oo" into eyes.

Make a motif around the dot of an "i"

Decorate the first letter of your name.

25

Flowers and leaves

You can gather flowers or leaves at any time of year, but if you want to press and keep them, do it on a dry day.

Only collect common types of flowers from your garden. Wild ones may be rare or protected species.

Pressing

You need: some heavy books; blotting paper; newspaper.

1. Place a few sheets of newspaper on one book. Put a sheet of blotting paper on top.

2. Arrange the leaves or flowers on the blotting paper so that they don't touch.

3. Cover with more blotting paper and newspaper. Put heavy books on top and leave for five weeks.

Making pictures

Bookmark   *Card*   *Gift tag*

Once your leaves and flowers are ready, you can use them to make pictures for cards, gift tags or bookmarks. First cut a shape for the thing you want to make, from thin cardboard.

Add a hole for ribbon.

1. Arrange the pressed leaves and flowers on one side of the cardboard.

2. Glue each piece in place. Cover with book covering film. Trim the edges.

Tips

• Press thick and thin flowers separately.
• Snip off thick parts of the stem before pressing.
• Check large flowers after a week. Turn them over carefully.
• Grasses are already quite dry. To flatten, put them under a mat where you walk.

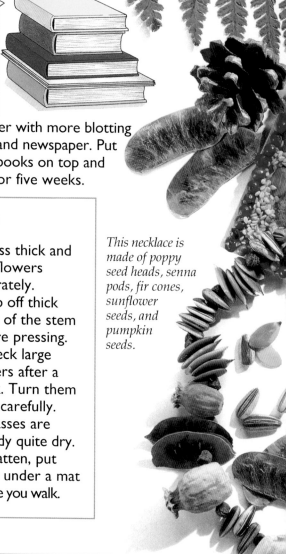

This necklace is made of poppy seed heads, senna pods, fir cones, sunflower seeds, and pumpkin seeds.

Seeds

Many plants have interesting seeds. Use tiny ones to make a picture. Larger ones can be strung together like beads for a necklace or bracelet.

Poppy seed heads and fir cones look good sprayed silver or gold.

Conkers

"Conkers" is a game you can play with the fruits of horse chestnut trees. Look for them at the end of the summer. Here's how to play:

1. Ask an adult to make a hole with a skewer.

2. Thread through a boot lace. Tie a knot in the end.

3. Take turns hitting each other's horse chestnut. The first chestnut to split, loses.

To make your horse chestnut tougher, bake it in the oven, or paint and varnish it.

For the necklace

1. Choose your seeds and lay them out in the order you want to use them.

2. Cut a piece of thread to fit over your head easily. Then thread a needle with it.

3. Pierce each seed carefully with the needle and pull along the thread.

4. When you have added all your beads, tie the ends of the thread together.

For the bracelet

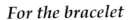

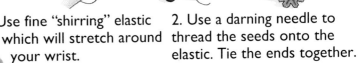

1. Use fine "shirring" elastic which will stretch around your wrist.

2. Use a darning needle to thread the seeds onto the elastic. Tie the ends together.

Coins

Coins have been around for nearly 3,000 years. The Ancient Greeks invented them and the Romans used them too. You can see these ancient coins in some museums.

The thing about collecting coins is that you can do it as cheaply or as expensively as you want, depending on what you decide to collect. The hobby is called numismatics.

Old, used coins

Shiny new coins

Coins of different values are different sizes.

Each side of a coin is different.

What to collect

You could start by studying a selection of coins in your money box. See how many different types there are. Always pick the coin in best condition for your collection.

There are several different ways you could specialize. You might decide to collect coins from just your own country, or coins of one type of metal. You could choose one coin and look for examples with different dates.

If you are interested in the pictures on coins, look at coins from all over the world. There's a huge variety. As your collection grows, you could even specialize in just one type of picture, such as animals or transportation.

Coins with animals

Not all coins are round. Look for unusual shapes.

Commemorative coins mark a special event.

Coins with holes

Where to get coins

Ask your parents or grandparents if they have any old coins. They may have kept some that have gone out of circulation. This is when people stop using them to buy things because new ones have been introduced.

For foreign coins, find out if anyone you know is going abroad. When they return they can only change notes back into their own currency, so they may have some spare coins that you could have.

Old coins are often replaced by smaller ones.

Caring for coins

Always look for coins that are in good condition. Never clean or polish them. It can damage the detail and devalue them.

Try not to touch your coins too often. Pick them up by the edges with your finger and thumb when you need to handle them.

You can buy albums full of transparent pages with little pockets specially for coins, or frame your best coins as shown below.

Frame coins of one country together, or just pick the ones you like best.

Framing your coins

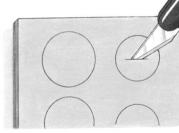

You need: a small clip-frame with glass; two pieces of bright felt, cut to the same size as the frame; a piece of thin cardboard, cut to the same size as the frame; a pencil; glue stick; a craft knife.

1. Put aside one piece of felt and glue the other piece to the cardboard. Leave it to dry.

2. Turn it felt-side-down and arrange your coins on the cardboard. Draw around each one.

3. Keeping your fingers out of the way, pierce the middle of a coin shape with the craft knife.

Backing board

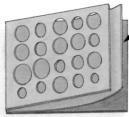

4. Using the craft knife very carefully, cut around the pencil line. It is easiest if you do a little piece at a time.

5. Cut holes for each coin. Turn felt-side-up and try the coins for size. If necessary trim the holes a little more.

6. Open the frame. Place the uncut felt on the backing board, then the cut piece, felt-side-up, on top.

7. Put your coins in place, add the glass on top and close the frame. Polish the glass and hang on the wall.

Other ideas

Bottles

Bottles come in all shapes and sizes. You can collect tall ones, small ones, plain or tinted glass.

Next time you are in the supermarket, take a look at all the products that come in bottles. See how many different shapes and shades of glass there are.

Plain glass bottles look good filled with sand, tinted water or beads. Line them up along a window sill or book shelf. Perfume often comes in small, unusual bottles. If you collect just these, you could display them on some miniature shelves like the ones on page 20.

In the past people used bottles to store all sorts of things. You can still find these bottles in junk shops or at craft fairs. Some have the name of the product written on the glass.

Refrigerator magnets

You don't have to display these on a refrigerator. They will stick to all kinds of other things made of metal such as a desk lamp or a metal tray, like the round one on the left in the photograph.

Teddy bears

These cuddly toys are a real collectors' item. Old ones can be very valuable, so hang on to yours.

Hats

Why not have a different one for every day of the month? When you are not wearing them, hang them on picture hooks on your bedroom wall.

Egg cups

Egg cups are quite common in Britain but in many other countries they are unusual. Look for different shapes or ones with funny features.

Salt and pepper

Salt and pepper pots or shakers nearly always come in pairs, so try to find both halves. Sometimes the pepper and salt are the same, like the boots in the photograph. Sometimes they are different, like the man and his hut.

Collecting on a theme

Some people collect anything to do with one animal, person or subject. In the photograph there is a collection of fish things: mobiles, pictures, key rings, mugs, etc. You could collect cat or horse things instead, or things about a singer or sports personality.

Boxes and tins

Boxes and tins are useful to store other collections in but many are pretty enough to collect for themselves. Some old tins are quite sought-after and fairly expensive. Look for ones with nice pictures.

Books

Old books are often quite cheap in second-hand shops. The best ones have leather bindings and marbled inside pages. Some have lovely illustrations.

You can collect new books too: ones by the same author or illustrator, or books of one series. Books that come in series are sometimes numbered so that you can build a complete set.

Cacti

These weird-looking plants grow in hot or dry places that other plants can't survive in. They still need looking after though, so you will need to learn how to feed and water them.

Snowstorms

You often find these in souvenir shops. You could collect one every time you visit a new place.

With special thanks to:

Julietta Edgar, the Royal Mail Collectors Club; Val Brown, the Junior & International Fonecard Collectors Club; Frank Setchfield, the Badge Collectors Circle; Sam McCarthy Fox, the Marble Board of Control; John Mussell, Editor of Coin News; Susannah van Rose for advice on fossils and pebbles and Jan Light for advice on shells.

Every effort has been made to seek permission for all material photographed in this book and we would like to acknowledge the following for their help:

The Royal Mail, La Poste Française, Swiss Posts, Australia Post and Belgian Post for permission to reproduce stamps; The Exclusive Card Co. Ltd., Images and Editions, London Zoo, J. Arthur Dixon - photography by Vic Guy and Tony Wiles, Beric Tempest, Mayfair Cards of London (Tel: 0181 570 7458), Chuck Theodore/Rivendell art photography, Inga Spence/Holt Studios, Panorama Holiday Group, and Bob Croxford for permission to use their postcards; Mercury Communications and British Telecom for permission to use their Telephone cards; the Big Badge Company and London Emblem plc. for permission to use their badges.